# Dittoheads
# Little Instruction Book

*Dittoheads Little Instruction Book*
ISBN 1-57757-175-4
Copyright © 1996 by Trade Life

Published by Trade Life
P.O. Box 55325
Tulsa, OK  74155

# Dittoheads
# Little Instruction Book

**" DITTO "**

**"W**e hold these truths to be self-evident, that all men are created equal; that they are endowed by their Creator with certain inalienable rights; that among these are life, liberty, and the pursuit of happiness. That, to secure these rights, governments are instituted among men, deriving their just powers from the consent of the governed. **"**

THOMAS JEFFERSON

❝ It's time we reduced the
federal budget and left
the family budget alone. ❞

•

RONALD REAGAN

❝ I believe in the individual, in less
government so as to allow that
individual maximum freedom
to create and achieve. ❞

•

RUSH LIMBAUGH

"With my own ability, I cannot succeed, without the sustenance of Divine Providence, and of the great free, happy and intelligent people. Without these I cannot hope to succeed; with them, I cannot fail. "

**" DITTO "**

ABRAHAM LINCOLN

❝ The course of unbalanced budgets
is the road to ruin. ❞

•

HERBERT HOOVER


❝ The accounts of the United States
ought to be, and may be made, as
simple as those of a common farmer,
and capable of being understood
by common farmers. ❞

•

THOMAS JEFFERSON

" **A**mong the great evils of welfarism is that it transforms the individual from a dignified, industrious, self-reliant, spiritual being into a dependent animal creature without his knowing it. "

**" DITTO "**

BARRY GOLDWATER

**" One man with courage
makes a majority. "**

•

ANDREW JACKSON

**" In government, the sin of pride
manifests itself in the recurring
delusion that things are
under control. "**

•

GEORGE WILL

66 **And let us with caution indulge the supposition that morality can be maintained without religion. Whatever may be conceded to the influence of refined education on minds of peculiar structure, reason and experience both forbid us to expect that national morality can prevail in exclusion of religious principle.** 99

**" DITTO "**

GEORGE WASHINGTON

" **Ditto** "

" **W** e do not need to get good laws to restrain bad people. We need to get good people to restrain bad laws. "

G. K. CHESTERTON

❝ Neither a free economy nor a strong national defense can be sustained without the Judeo-Christian bedrock. ❞

•

GARY BAUER

❝ Let us humbly commit our righteous cause to the great Lord of the Universe. Let us joyfully leave our concerns in the hands of Him who raises up and puts down the empires and kingdoms of the earth as He pleases. ❞

•

JOHN HANCOCK

"**H**old fast to the Bible as the sheet-anchor of your liberties; write its precepts in your hearts and practice them in your lives. To the influence of this book we are indebted for all the progress made in true civilization and to this we must look as our guide in the future. "

**" DITTO "**

ULYSSES S. GRANT

❝ The responsibility of the judiciary is to uphold the Constitution, not rewrite it. ❞

•

BARRY GOLDWATER

❝ The highest glory of the American Revolution was this; it connected in one indissoluble bond, the principles of the civil government with the principles of Christianity. From the day of the Declaration the American people were bound by the laws of God. ❞

•

JOHN QUINCY ADAMS

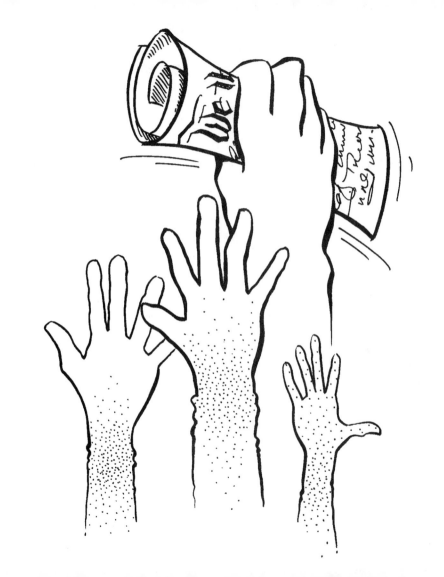

**"Goodness without wisdom always accomplishes evil."**

•

ROBERT HEINLEIN

**"If I knew that a man was coming to my house with the conscious design of doing me good, I should run for my life."**

•

HENRY DAVID THOREAU

**"It** would be peculiarly improper to omit, in this official act, my fervent supplication to that Almighty Being, who rules over the universe, who presides in the council of nations, and whose providential aid can supply every human defect, that His benediction may consecrate to the liberties and happiness of the people of the United States... Every step by which they have advanced seems to have been distinguished by some providential agency. We ought to be no less persuaded that the propitious smiles of Heaven can never be expected on a nation that disregards the eternal rules of order and right which Heaven itself has ordained. **"**

**" DITTO "**

GEORGE WASHINGTON

**❝When you punish people for engaging in certain behavior, that behavior is deterred. So to punish the successful, for example, with confiscatory taxes is to take aim at hard work and productivity. ❞**

•

RUSH LIMBAUGH

**❝Now that American values have prevailed in Eastern Europe, we should work to see to it that the same values prevail in Washington D.C. ❞**

•

WILLIAM J. BENNETT

" A Conservative is a Liberal with
a daughter in high school. "

•

GARY BAUER

" When you break the big laws,
you do not get liberty,
you do not even get anarchy.
You get the small laws. "

•

G. K. CHESTERTON

66 **I**s life so dear, or peace so sweet, as to be purchased at the price of chains and slavery? Forbid it, Almighty God! I know not what course others may take, but as for me: give me liberty or give me death! 99

**" DITTO "**

PATRICK HENRY

" Government is not the solution
to our problem.
Government is the problem. "

•

RONALD REAGAN

" Government is but a tool.
If ever we come to the place
where our tools determine what jobs
we can or cannot do, and by what
means, then nary a fortnight shall
pass in which new freedoms shall be
wrested from us straightway. "

•

HENRY CABOT LODGE

**"We desperately need to engage in the architecture of souls."**

•

WILLIAM J. BENNETT

**"People in public life have a responsibility to behave in a certain way that can be respected and emulated."**

•

HOWARD PHILLIPS

" **O**f all the tyrannies, a tyranny sincerely expressed for the good of its victims may be the most oppressive. It may be better to live under robber barons than under omnipotent busybodies. "

" DITTO "

C. S. LEWIS

**" DITTO "**

**"C**hristmas is a time when kids tell Santa what they want and adults pay for it. Deficits are when adults tell the government what they want — and their kids pay for it. **"**

RICHARD LAMM

**"When families fail, society fails. "**

•

DAN QUAYLE

**" There are those who would say, you cannot legislate morality.**

**On the contrary, morality is the only thing that you can legislate.**

**That's what legislation is: the legal codification of some moral standard. "**

•

D. JAMES KENNEDY

" **A**lmost nothing is as important as almost everything in Washington is made to appear, and the importance of a Washington event is apt to be inversely proportional to the attention it receives. "

**" DITTO "**

GEORGE WILL

❝ The nation should be ruled by the Ten Commandments. ❞

•

THEODORE ROOSEVELT

❝ No man can be a sound lawyer in this land who is not well read in the ethics of Moses and the virtues of Jesus. ❞

•

FISHER AMES

"If an unfriendly foreign power had attempted to impose on America a mediocre educational system, it could not have devised one worse than the one we presently have. "

•

JESSE HELMS

"The public schools of today sadly demonstrate an arrogance of power, a compulsion to control the minds and behavior of children, and a pervasive hostility toward parents. "

•

PHYLLIS SCHLAFLY

66 **It** won't matter how many bills we pass to balance the budget. It won't matter how many times we pass the flat tax or sales tax or any other economic reform. We will still go over the brink. Because what we really need to restore is the balance of our judgment and the balance of our moral will. 99

**" DITTO "**

ALAN KEYES

**"A Liberal is a Conservative who hasn't been mugged yet. "**

•

FRANK RIZZO

**"Collecting more taxes than is absolutely necessary is legalized robbery. "**

•

CALVIN COOLIDGE

"In politics, all that glitters
is sold as gold. "

•

OGDEN NASH

"The world has always been betrayed
by decent men with bad ideals. "

•

SYDNEY J. HARRIS

"There are twenty-seven specific complaints against the British Crown set forth in the Declaration of Independence. To modern ears they still sound reasonable. They still sound reasonable in large part, because so many of them can be leveled against the present federal government of the United States."

**" DITTO "**

P. J. O'ROURKE

" The laws of gravity apply to America
as well as to other nations —
so do the laws of economics.
Too bad Congress doesn't act like it. "

•

HOWARD PHILLIPS

" There is something about a
Republican that you can only stand
him for just so long. And on the other
hand, there is something about
a Democrat that you can't stand
him for quite that long. "

•

WILL ROGERS

" I will not stand for having animals
assigned rights and privileges
that many human beings
don't yet enjoy. "

•

RUSH LIMBAUGH

" When I suggested to my dog that
animals had rights, he laughed out
loud. To this day I don't think he
respects me the way he did before I
had that conversation with him. "

•

RUSH LIMBAUGH

"The American dream is not just about money and material advancement. It is a dream of freedom."

**" DITTO "**

ALAN KEYES

**" L**iberty: Civilization's highest concept. **"**

NORMAN SCHWARTZKOPF

**"It is often so with institutions already undermined; they are at their most splendid external phase when they are ripe for downfall. "**

•

HILAIRE BELLOC

**"Value-free education may be just another name for an education approach that makes people unfit for freedom. "**

•

ALAN KEYES

66 **If you're going to sin, sin against God, not the bureaucracy. God will forgive you, but the bureaucracy won't.** 99

**" DITTO "**

HYMAN RICKOVER

" Has America become a country where classroom discussion of the Ten Commandments is impermissible, but teacher instructions in safe sodomy are to be mandatory? "

•

PATRICK BUCHANAN

" No tyrant has ever effectually conquered and subjugated a people whose liberties and public virtue were founded on the Word of God. "

•

GARDINER SPRING

" It is indeed possible that steps to relieve misery can create misery. The most troubling aspect of social policy toward the poor in late twentieth century America is not how much is costs, but what it has bought. "

**" DITTO "**

CHARLES MURRAY

❝ One of the things liberals are famous for is manufacturing problems with their wacky theories, then proposing even wackier theories to solve the problems they have created. ❞

•

RUSH LIMBAUGH


❝ Do-gooders are the world's most notorious do-baders. ❞

•

TRISTIAN GYLBERD

**" An unlimited power to tax involves, necessarily, the power to destroy. "**

•

DANIEL WEBSTER

**" The income tax has made more liars out of the American people than golf has. "**

•

WILL ROGERS

"**G**od is a Republican and Santa Claus is a democrat. God is an elderly, or at any rate, middle-aged male, a stern fellow, patriarchal rather than paternal and a great believer in rules and regulations. He holds men strictly accountable for their actions.

Santa Claus is another matter. He's cute. He's nonthreatening. He's always cheerful. And he loves animals. He may know who's been naughty and who's been nice, but he never does anything about it.

**" DITTO "**

Santa Claus is preferable to God in every way but one: There is no such thing as Santa Claus. **"**

P. J. O'ROURKE

**"A Liberal is one who loves the world, but hates his neighbor. "**

•

WILLIS PLAYER

**"Instead of teaching children the three 'R's — reading, writing and arithmetic — the public schools are enthusiastically indoctrinating them with the four 'R's — reversionism, revisionism, reprobations, and radicalism. "**

•

MICHAEL HARLINSON

"**A**ll across this country, the school curriculum has been invaded by psychological conditioning programs which not only take up time sorely needed for intellectual development, but also promote an emotionalized and anti-intellectual way of responding to the challenges facing every individual and every society. Worst of all, the psycho-therapeutic curriculum systematically undermines the parent-child relationship and the shared values which make society possible. "

**" DITTO "**

THOMAS SOWELL

**" The current tax code
is a daily mugging. "**

•

RONALD REAGAN

**" The worst thing in the world,
next to anarchy, is government. "**

•

HENRY WARD BEECHER

**❝Tyranny is too much government. ❞**

•

CLEON SKOUSEN

**❝Religious liberty is so blended with civil, that if one falls it is not expected that the other will continue. ❞**

•

CHARLES TURNER

"**O**ne of the best ways to get yourself a reputation as a dangerous citizen these days is to go about repeating the very phrases which our founding fathers used in their struggle for independence. "

**" DITTO "**

C. A. BEARD

" There isn't a conviction I hold that makes liberals livid more quickly than this one: America is the greatest country on Earth and in history, still abounding with untapped opportunity for ordinary citizens. "

•

RUSH LIMBAUGH

" Any man who actually wants to be president, probably is not qualified. "

•

JOHN QUINCY ADAMS

" Indifference in questions of importance is no amiable quality. "

SAMUEL JOHNSON

" All the evils in our now extensive catalogue flow from a falsified picture of the world which, for our immediate concern, results in an inability to interpret current happenings. "

RICHARD WEAVER

66 **The contention that the civil government should at its option intrude into and exercise control over the family and the household is a great and pernicious error.** 99

**" DITTO "**

VINCENZO PECCI

**"P**ublic schools in America are essentially monopolies. They are financed by compulsory taxation, enjoy a captive audience of students thanks to compulsory-attendance laws, and — in most cities — assign students to schools according to where they live. Parents who are dissatisfied with the quality of education their children are receiving must either move to an affluent area, where schools are often better, or send their children to private schools. If they choose the latter, parents must pay twice for their children's education: once in property taxes and again in tuition. **"**

**" DITTO "**

JAMES BENNETT AND
THOMAS DILORENZO

"Civil liberty is not freedom from restraint. Men may be wisely and benevolently checked, and yet be free. No man has a right to act as he thinks fit, irrespective of the wishes and interests of others. This would be exemption from all law, and from the wholesome influence of social institutions. Heaven itself would not be free, if this were freedom. No created being holds any such liberty as this, by a divine warrant. The spirit of subordination, so far from being inconsistent with liberty, is inseparable from it."

**" DITTO "**

GARDINER SPRING

**❝ It is impossible to rightly govern without God and the Bible ❞**

GEORGE WASHINGTON

**❝ The men who established this government had faith in God and sublimely trusted Him. They besought His counsel and advice in every step of their progress. And so it has been ever since...our rulers may not always be observers of the outward forms of religion, but we have never had a president, from Washington to Harrison,who publicly avowed infidelity, or scoffed at the faith of the masses of our people. ❞**

WILLIAM MCKINLEY

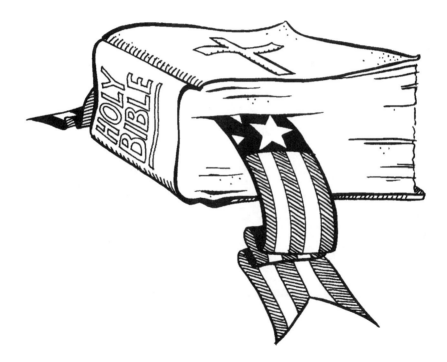

**❝ Modernism is in essence a provincialism, since it declines to look beyond the horizon of the moment. ❞**

•

RICHARD WEAVER

**❝ The only surety for a permanent foundation of virtue is religion. Let this important truth be engraved upon your heart. ❞**

•

ABIGAIL ADAMS

" **R**eligion and liberty are the meat and the drink of the body politic. Withdraw one of them and it languishes, consumes, and dies. Without religion we may possibly retain the freedom of savages, bears, and wolves, but not the freedom of New England. If our religion were gone, our state of society would perish with it, and nothing would be left. "

**" DITTO "**

TIMOTHY DWIGHT

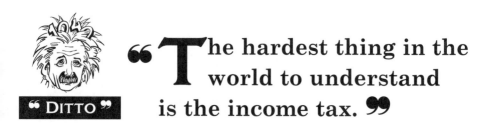

**"The** hardest thing in the world to understand is the income tax. **"**

ALBERT EINSTEIN

**"We get more of what we pay for and less of what we tax. "**

•

ALLAN C. CARLSON

**"The enemies of the future are always the very nicest people. "**

•

CHRISTOPHER MORLEY

**66 It is natural to mean well, when only abstracted ideas of virtue are proposed to the mind, and no particular passion turns us aside from rectitude; and so willing is every man to flatter himself, that the difference between approving laws and obeying them is frequently forgotten. 99**

**" Ditto "**

SAMUEL JOHNSON

" To establish the fact of decadence is the most pressing duty of our time. "

•

RICHARD WEAVER

" I tell people, 'Don't kill off all the liberals. Leave enough around so we can have two on every campus — living fossils — so we will never forget what these people stood for.' "

•

RUSH LIMBAUGH

" The hand of Divine Providence was never more plainly visible in the affairs of men than in the framing and adopting of the Constitution. "

•

ANDREW JOHNSON

" The foundations of our society and our government rest so much on the teachings of the Bible that it would be difficult to support them if faith in these teachings would cease to be practically universal in our country. "

•

CALVIN COOLIDGE

" **N**eedless taxes are not for the good, but the misery of the citizenry, tending to reduce them to poverty and distress; and may therefore be justly considered as wanton undisguised oppression, to support the pride, ambition, extravagance of a few grandees. "

" DITTO "

ROBERT ROSS

**❝ The best things in life invariably cost us something. We must sacrifice to attain them, to achieve them, to keep them, even to enjoy them. ❞**

•

JAMES Q. WILSON

**❝ Cutting the heart out of our defenses is roughly like canceling all your fire insurance because you did not have a fire last year. ❞**

•

CASPAR WEINBERGER

" **N**o human society has ever been able to maintain both order and freedom, both cohesiveness and liberty apart from the moral precepts of the Christian Religion applied and accepted by all the classes. Should our Republic ever forget this fundamental precept of governance, men are certain to shed their responsibilities for licentiousness and this great experiment will then surely be doomed. "

" DITTO "

JOHN JAY

**" DITTO "**

**"There is no trick to being a humorist when you have the whole government working for you. "**

WILL ROGERS

**❝ The tasks of family in society lie outside the government's jurisdiction. With those it is not to meddle — at the risk of stealing away all our liberties. ❞**

•

ABRAHAM KUYPER

**❝ The primary means of cultural renewal in this civilization is not the government, it is communities, churches, schools, families, and businesses. ❞**

•

WILLIAM BENNETT

"Somehow, our whole approach to teaching and learning has gone awry. Do you sometimes have an uneasy suspicion that the product of modern educational methods is less good than he or she might be at disentangling fact from opinion and the proven from the plausible? Although we often succeed in teaching our pupils subjects, we fail lamentably on the whole in teaching them how to think. They learn everything except the art of learning."

**" DITTO "**

DOROTHY SAYERS

**"Ditto"**

**"If you want a friend in Washington, buy a dog."**

HARRY TRUMAN

**" You can't even trust the dogs
in this town. "**

•

CLARENCE THOMAS

**" If it were not for government, we
should have nothing left to laugh at. "**

•

NICHOLAS CHAMFORT

" **T**hat it does not matter what a man believes is a statement heard on every side today. The statement carries a fearful implication. The statement really means that it does not matter what a man believes so long as he does not take his beliefs seriously. "

RICHARD WEAVER

66 Two characteristics of government are that it cannot do anything quickly, and that it never knows when to quit. 99

•

**GEORGE STIGLER**

66 It has become fashionable to dismiss almost any significant attempt to change things as single-issue-politics. Politicians, apparently, aren't supposed to emphasize anything, but are supposed to offer a big menu of small snacks. 99

•

**JACK KEMP**

**❝Some talk in quarto volumes and act in pamphlets. ❞**

•

JOHN PYM

**❝The greatest political storm flutters only a fringe of humanity. ❞**

•

G. K. CHESTERTON

" **M**y story is nothing more than an example of the Original American Ethic: hard work, overcoming obstacles, triumphing over enormous odds, the pioneer spirit. These things, my friends — not such vacuous symbolic gestures as wearing ribbons on lapels or government intrusion into every aspect of our lives — are what built this country. "

" DITTO "

RUSH LIMBAUGH

" Economic and material gains are no compensation for social and moral ills. "

•

GERTRUDE HIMMELFARB

" Statesmen may plan and speculate for liberty, but it is Religion and Morality alone which can establish the Principles upon which Freedom can securely stand. "

•

JOHN ADAMS

" **H**ere richly, with ridiculous display, the politician's corpse was laid away. While all his acquaintance sneered and slanged, I wept; for I had longed to see him hanged. "

" DITTO "

HILAIRE BELLOC

"Ditto"

"**A** new deal implies that I'm the dealer and you get the cards. We want a new partnership. A partnership implies we both have responsibility. "

NEWT GINGRICH

**"Where tyranny begins, government ends."**

•

SAMUEL WEST

**"Every considerate friend of civil liberty, in order to be consistent with himself, must be the friend of the Bible."**

•

GARDINER SPRING

**"The first thing a man will do for his ideals is lie. "**

**JOSEPH SCHUMPTER**

" The most healing of medicines,
unduly administered, becomes
the most deadly of poisons. "

•

JOHN QUINCY ADAMS

" Political advertising is the
modern substitute for argument;
its function is to make the
worse appear the better. "

•

GEORGE SANTAYANA

"**G**overnment does not produce wealth: it consumes it, squanders it, and redistributes it. Ultimately, that is still theft even if it's done in broad daylight, in elegant surroundings, by majority vote. "

**" DITTO "**

HOWARD PHILLIPS

"Ditto"

" **T**he American people are fine. Washington is not. The patient is in better shape than the doctor. "

WILLIAM J. BENNETT

**" DITTO "**

" The essence of government is force: whatever its end, its means is compulsion. Government forces people to do what they would not otherwise choose to do, or it forces them to refrain from doing what they otherwise do. So, when we say, "Government should do x," we are really saying, "People should be forced to do x." It should be obvious that force should be used only for the most serious reasons, such as preventing and punishing violence. The frivolous, improper, or excessive use of force is wrong. We used to call it tyranny. Unfortunately, too many people think that calling for the government to do x is merely a way of saying that x is desirable. And so we are increasingly forced to do things that are not genuine social duties but merely good ideas. The result is that the role of state coercion in our lives grows greater and greater. "

Joseph Sobran

**"The Founding Fathers, who liberals fraudulently identify as their soul mates, incorporated into the Constitution the principle of equality of opportunity, not equality of result. "**

**" DITTO "**

RUSH LIMBAUGH

"Government is not reason, it is not eloquence — it is force. "

GEORGE WASHINGTON

"A Liberal is a man too broadminded to take his own side in a quarrel. "

ROBERT FROST

66 **The legions of well-intentioned but smug, educated elites have agreed in advance to reject thousands of years of inherited wisdom, values, habit, custom, and insight and replace this heritage with their official utopian vision of the perfect society.** 99

**" DITTO "**

WILLIAM GAIRDNER

" Conservatism is the politics
of reality. "

•

RICHARD ARMEY

"What the liberals are really afraid
of is not the right wing,
but the eternal truth that the
traditional family is still the
best way to live. "

•

PHYLLIS SCHLAFLY

DITTOHEADS LITTLE INSTRUCTION BOOK

**" The greatest destroyer of peace is abortion, because if a mother can kill her own child, what is left for me to kill you and you to kill me? There is nothing between. "**

•

MOTHER TERESA

**" A nation that kills its unborn children cannot teach its citizens to love one another. "**

•

MOTHER TERESA

" **W**hen it comes to deciding whether we shall stand by the great principle that declares that all human beings are created equal and endowed by their Creator with the right to life, there is no choice for silence. "

**ALAN KEYES**

" DITTO "

" Ditto "

**"I** belong to no organized political party —
I'm a democrat. **"**

WILL ROGERS

**" Child care is a family issue —
not a government issue. "**

•

ROBERT J. DOLE

**" The Liberals have put on political
trench coats and dark glasses
and slipped their platform into
a plain brown wrapper. "**

•

RONALD REAGAN

"Religion, or the duty which we owe to our Creator and the manner of discharging it, can be directed only by reason and conviction, not by force or violence; and therefore all men are equally entitled to the free exercise of religion, according to the dictates of conscience. It is the mutual duty of all to practice Christian forbearance, love, and charity towards each other."

PATRICK HENRY

**" Ditto "**

" **N**o people ought to feel greater obligations to celebrate the goodness of the Great Disposer of events and of the destiny of nations than the people of the United States. His kind providence originally conducted them to one of the best portions of the dwelling place allotted for the great family of the human race. He protected and cherished them under all the difficulties and trials to which they were exposed in their early days. Under His fostering care their habits, their sentiments, and their pursuits prepared them for a transition in due time to a state of independence and self-government. "

JAMES MADISON

"When was the last time you read an article about poverty, about crime, about the problems in our educational system that didn't point to one overriding truth: that every single one of those problems is tied to the disintegration of the marriage-based, two parent family the most important moral institution in the land? When are we going to wake up? The moral problems of this country are its practical problems."

" DITTO "

ALAN KEYES

❝ I said to my Liberal friend that we are fundamentally the same. I spend money like it's my money and you spend money like it's my money. ❞

•

RICHARD ARMEY

❝ The intelligent man, when he pays taxes, certainly does not believe that he is making a prudent and productive investment of his money; on the contrary, he feels that he is being mulcted in an excessive amount for services that, in the main, are useless to him, and that, in substantial part, are downright inimical to him. He sees them as purely predatory and useless. ❞

•

H. L. MENCKEN

❝Giving is the vital impulse and moral center of capitalism. ❞

•

GEORGE GILDER

❝The left is very smart.
They always conceal their greed
for power in the language of love. ❞

•

NEWT GINGRICH

"Since the time of Bacon the world has been running away from, rather than toward, first principles, so that, on the verbal level, we see fact substituted for truth."

" DITTO "

RICHARD WEAVER

" If men will not be governed by the Ten Commandments they shall be governed by the ten thousand commandments. "

G. K. CHESTERTON

" The only foundation for a republic is to be laid in Religion. Without this there can be no virtue, and without virtue there can be no liberty, and liberty is the object and life of all republican governments. "

BENJAMIN RUSH

"We are gripped by an aching
Angst, the social equivalent
of postpartum blues."

•

STEVE FORBES

"All heaven and earth resound with
that subtle and delicately balanced
truth that the old paths are the
best paths after all."

•

J. C. RYLE

66 **A contempt of the monuments and the wisdom of the past, may be justly reckoned one of the reigning follies of these days, to which pride and idleness have equally contributed.** 99

**" DITTO "**

SAMUEL JOHNSON

"DITTO"

**"T**he most terrifying words in the English language are: I'm from the government and I'm here to help.**"**

RONALD REAGAN

**" Ditto "**

" The great intellectual tradition that comes down to us from the past was never interrupted or lost through such trifles as the sack of Rome, the triumph of Attila, or all the barbarian invasions of the Dark Ages. It was lost after the introduction of printing, the discovery of America, the coming of the marvels of technology, the establishment of universal education, and all the enlightenment of the modern world. It was there, if anywhere, that there was lost or impatiently snapped the long thin delicate thread that had descended from distant antiquity; the thread of that unusual human hobby: The habit of thinking. "

G. K. CHESTERTON

66 **I**'m not prejudiced. I'm postjudiced. Postjudice is the compliment that common sense pays to experience. 99

**" DITTO "**

WILLIAM F. BUCKLEY, JR.

**❝Integrity is the heart of a free society. A society without integrity has cancer at its heart. ❞**

•

NEWT GINGRICH

**❝The only government bureaucracy that is shrinking in size is the one that was successful in, not to mention essential to, the preservation of our liberty — the military. ❞**

•

RUSH LIMBAUGH

**" The great tragedy of our day is that truth is not politically correct. "**

•

PAT ROBERTSON

**" The ultimate purpose of our foreign policy must be to protect the liberty of the people of the United States. "**

•

ROBERT TAFT

## 66 **C**haracter is the only secure foundation of the state. 99

CALVIN COOLIDGE

**" The family is the original Department of Health, Education and Welfare. "**

·

WILLIAM J. BENNETT

**" That government is best which governs least. "**

·

HENRY DAVID THOREAU

**" Ditto "**

" **F**ifty years ago it would have seemed quite impossible in America that an individual be granted boundless freedom with no purpose but simply for the satisfaction of his whims. The defense of individual rights has reached such extremes as to make society as a whole defenseless. It is time to defend, not so much human rights, as human obligations. "

ALEKSANDR SOLZHENITSYN

66 **I sought for the greatness and genius of America in her commodious harbors and her ample rivers, and it was not there; in her fertile fields and boundless prairies, and it was not here; in her rich mines and her vast world commerce, and it was not there. Not until I went to the churches of America and heard her pulpits aflame with righteousness did I understand the secret of her genius and power. America is great because she is good and if America ever ceases to be good, America will cease to be great.** 99

**" DITTO "**

**ALEXIS DE TOCQUEVILLE**

" **W**e must beware of reducing society to the state or the state to society. For the state to take over the tasks of society and of the family is outside its jurisdiction and competency. "

**" DITTO "**

ABRAHAM KUYPER

66 **I**n this actual world, a churchless community, a community where men have abandoned and scoffed at, or ignored their Christian duties, is a community on the rapid down-grade. 99

**" DITTO "**

THEODORE ROOSEVELT

**" DITTO "**

" **T**he Constitution is not an instrument for government to restrain the people, it is an instrument for the people to restrain the government — lest it come to dominate our lives and interests. "

PATRICK HENRY

**"You can't get ahead while you're getting even."**

•

RICHARD ARMEY

**"We don't have money problems. We have moral problems."**

•

ALAN KEYES

"**D**espite its historic political and economic triumphs, the American Republic is entering its own time of reckoning, an hour of truth that will not be delayed. It is nearing the climax of a generation-long cultural revolution, or crisis of cultural authority. "

**" DITTO "**

OS GUINNESS

" Ditto "

**" Balancing the budget is like going to heaven. Everybody wants to do it, but nobody wants to do what you have to do to get there. "**

PHIL GRAMM

" It is quite clear from the Declaration of Independence that when you attempt to separate God from America, you separate the people from their freedom. "

•

ALAN KEYES

" It is impossible for most politicians to change the culture of Washington, because they are the culture of Washington. "

•

LAMAR ALEXANDER

66 The time will come when we entrust the conduct of our affairs to men who understand that their first duty as public officials is to divest themselves of the power they have been given. It will come when Americans decide to put the man in office who is pledged to enforce the Constitution and restore the Republic, who will proclaim in a campaign speech: I have little interest in streamlining government or in making it more efficient, for I mean to reduce its size. I do not undertake to promote welfare for I propose to extend freedom. My aim is not to pass laws but to repeal them. It is not to inaugurate new programs but to cancel old ones that do violence to the Constitution. 99

**" DITTO "**

BARRY GOLDWATER

**" DITTO "**

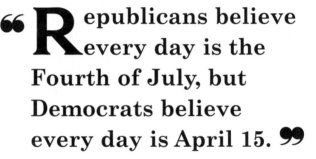

" **R**epublicans believe every day is the Fourth of July, but Democrats believe every day is April 15. "

RONALD REAGAN

" All Socialists are either dumb
or romantic. "

•

WILLIAM F. BUCKLEY

" Perhaps one of the most important
accomplishments of my
administration has been minding
my own business. "

•

CALVIN COOLIDGE

" **W**e have
succeeded in
demoralizing social
policy — divorcing it
from any moral criteria,
requirements, or even
expectations. "

**" DITTO "**

GERTRUDE HIMMELFARB

"We want to reach out to everyone in America. We'll give a helping hand up the ladder of responsibility, but there is no escalator. "

•

NEWT GINGRICH

"The definition of compassion is the number of people who no longer need government assistance. "

•

J. C. WATTS

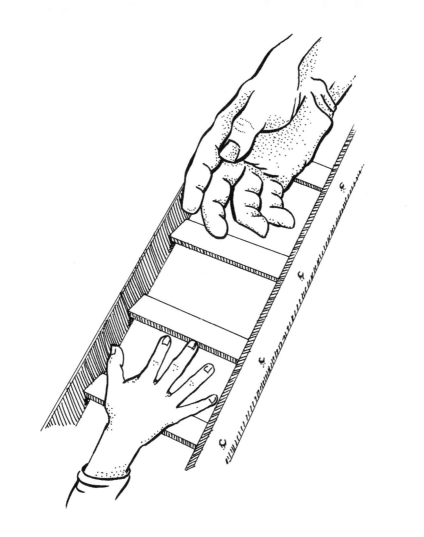

" Government always finds a need
for whatever money it gets. "

•

RONALD REAGAN

" A billion here, a billion there;
the first thing you know,
you're talking about real money. "

•

EVERETT DIRKSEN

**" We** have staked the whole future of American civilization, not upon the power of government, far from it. We have staked the future upon the capacity of each and all of us to govern ourselves, to sustain ourselves, according to the Ten Commandments of God. **"**

**" DITTO "**

JAMES MADISON

**" DITTO "**

**"The** philosophy of the classroom in one generation will be the philosophy of government in the next. **"**

ABRAHAM LINCOLN

> **"Bureaucracy is the technical embodiment of hell itself. "**
>
> •
>
> C. S. LEWIS

> **"Our peculiar security is in the possession of a written constitution. Let us not make it a blank paper by construction. "**
>
> •
>
> THOMAS JEFFERSON

66 **O**ur morality emanates from our Divine Creator, whose laws are not subject to amendment, modification, or rescission by man. 99

**" DITTO "**

RUSH LIMBAUGH

**" Ditto "**

**" P**olitics ought to be the part-time profession of every citizen who would protect the rights and privileges of free people. **"**

Dwight D. Eisenhower

# Other books by Trade Life:

*The Little Instruction Book*
*of Business Etiquette*

*The Little Book of Olympic Inspiration*

*How to Be the Man of Your Wife's Dreams*
*and Not Her Worst Nightmare*

*How to Be the Woman of Your Husband's*
*Dreams and Not His Worst Nightmare*